GREATNESS
Is Within Me!

A Teen's Guide To Journaling

by
Steve Viglione

27 South Munroe Terrace, Suite 4000
Boston, Massachusetts 02122

The author respects all persons' inherent right to believe as they choose. His intention is that this journal will serve as complimentary to each individual's background of faith.

God's Greatness Is Within Me! A Teen's Guide to Journaling.

Permission is granted to teachers, clergy and study groups to duplicate pages for writing exercises.

Quantity discounts given for churches, youth camps, bookstores and organizations. Please call 1-800-684-1313.

ISBN 0-9645224-2-X

"For Behold, the Kingdom of God is Within You."

–Luke 17:21

"Our deepest fear is not that we are inadequate. Our deepest fear is that we are powerful beyond measure. It is our light, not our darkness, that most frightens us. We ask ourselves, who am I to be brilliant, gorgeous, talented and fabulous? Actually, who are you *not* to be? You are a child of God. Your playing small doesn't serve the world. There's nothing enlightened about shrinking so that other people won't feel insecure around you. You were born to make manifest the Glory of God that is within us. It's not just in some of us; it's in everyone. And as we let our own light shine, we unconsciously give other people permission to do the same. As we are liberated from our own fear, our presence automatically liberates others."

— *Nelson Mandela*
Quote from His
1994 Inaugural Speech

Dedication

This journal is dedicated to you, today's teen.
As you write your story you will tap into
the inner strength inside you and become
more of the strong individual you are
intended to be. You will
be tapping into the infinite Greatness which is
within you already.
Always remember...
I believe in *you*.

"I can do all things through Christ who strengthens me."

–Philippians 4:13

Introduction

This journal was written especially for you, today's teen, because life is often very tough as a teenager. You may be experiencing issues in relationships, fears about becoming an adult, or difficulty in finding your true path, just to name a few.

To help keep you centered and focused, I encourage you to affirm this as often as possible:

God's Greatness Is Within Me!

Keep affirming it until you know this is the truth about who you are! After that, continue to say it to remind yourself of who you are, because all of us have days...*those* days where we may not feel so *Great*.

The truth is we are inseparable from an incredible *Greatness*. I call this Greatness *God*. We are always a part of God because we are God's wonderful creation. God is in all, over all and through all. Therefore, the Greatness of God is within us all. If you ever doubt this for a moment, simply think of how uniquely and intricately the world is designed- how everything lives together in perfect balance-how our bodies work and function.

God works through us in our daily lives through our minds, hearts and bodies, sustaining us. God works through who we are, what we do and who we interact with at every moment. This is all the proof you need to know *God is Great and God's Greatness Is Within You!*

Through the wonderful gift of faith, one can accomplish great things. A famous motivational speaker said, *"Believing is Seeing!"* and it is so true. There are those who must see to believe, but I ask you, how much good does that bring? How can that ever possibly build faith in ourselves or in God? How can we ever become *greater* ourselves or become more self-confident, if we have to see everything before we believe it?

In your approach to journaling, I welcome you to stretch and grow and become the truly remarkable person you really are. You will notice there are similar topics on each page throughout the book. This is done intentionally in order that you develop, and stay true to, your goals, dreams and visions. Approach them with love and passion. Practice patience, because *with God* these and all things are possible. Through belief and *with God* you will realize your true potential. I wholeheartedly support you in this.

Richest blessings,

God is Great. And God's Greatness is within me.

_____

_____

_____

_____

_____

_____

_____

_____

_____

_____

_____

_____

_____

_____

_____

_____

_____

_____

_____

_____

_____

_____

_____

_____

_____

_____

"Surely God is in thee..."

—Isaiah 45:14

I live for the Glory of God, and for the Divine Plan God has in store for me.

_____

_____

_____

_____

_____

_____

_____

_____

_____

_____

_____

_____

_____

_____

_____

_____

_____

_____

_____

_____

_____

_____

_____

_____

_____

"For I know the plans I have for you...they are plans for good and not for evil, to give you a future and a hope."

—Jeremiah 29:11

There is creative genius in me. I tap into its infinite supply and find it is forever expanding. I can use it anytime.

_____
_____
_____
_____
_____
_____
_____
_____
_____
_____
_____
_____
_____
_____
_____
_____
_____
_____
_____
_____
_____
_____
_____

"I and the Father are One."

—*John 10:30*

~ 3 ~

My thoughts and words have tremendous power. I choose them both carefully. They take me where I want to go.

_____

_____

_____

_____

_____

_____

_____

_____

_____

_____

_____

_____

_____

_____

_____

_____

_____

_____

_____

_____

_____

_____

"So shall my word be that goeth forth out of my mouth: it shall not return unto me void, but it shall accomplish that which I please."
—Isaiah 55:11

An eternal spring of Good flows forth from my life, healing, loving, blessing all with whom I meet and come in contact. I am a vehicle for Good.

_____
_____
_____
_____
_____
_____
_____
_____
_____
_____
_____
_____
_____
_____
_____
_____
_____
_____
_____
_____
_____
_____
_____
_____
_____
_____

"God, our God, has blessed us."

—Psalm 67:6

My days and nights are in Divine balance and order. There is perfect priority. God, the Greatness within me, knows exactly what to do next. I listen. I hear. I act.

_____
_____
_____
_____
_____
_____
_____
_____
_____
_____
_____
_____
_____
_____
_____
_____
_____
_____
_____
_____
_____
_____
_____
_____

"Put things in order."

—*2 Corinthians 13:11*

**Every beat of my heart proves the magnificence of life.
With such Majesty as evidence of love within me, I know
I am part of the true Greatness from which I was born.**

_____

_____

_____

_____

_____

_____

_____

_____

_____

_____

_____

_____

_____

_____

_____

_____

_____

_____

_____

_____

_____

_____

_____

_____

_____

*"Thine, O Lord, is the greatness, and the power, and the glory, and
the victory, and the majesty."*

—1 Chronicles 29:11

I love to read. The more I read the more I know. The
more I know the more I become. I am always receiving an
education. I am divinely guided in my thirst for knowledge.

_____

_____

_____

_____

_____

_____

_____

_____

_____

_____

_____

_____

_____

_____

_____

_____

_____

_____

_____

_____

_____

"I will instruct you and teach you the way you should go."
—Psalm 32:8

Many of the Great Achievers in life started without anything. They had everything inside. And so do I.

_____
_____
_____
_____
_____
_____
_____
_____
_____
_____
_____
_____
_____
_____
_____
_____
_____
_____
_____
_____
_____
_____
_____

"Through wisdom is a house built; and by understanding it is established."

—*Proverbs 24:3*

I talk to and learn from others who are doing exactly what I'd love to do. I learn more about things that interest me. Knowledge is power and it helps me realize my dreams.

_____
_____
_____
_____
_____
_____
_____
_____
_____
_____
_____
_____
_____
_____
_____
_____
_____
_____
_____
_____
_____
_____
_____
_____

"In all that they do, they prosper."

—*Psalm 1:3*

I am not in a race to have more than someone else. I am entitled to my own Good. God provides my Good with ease. I bless what others have and we are all blessed.

"I will heal them and reveal to them abundance of prosperity and security."

—Jeremiah 33:6

I am friendly and personable. I am a strong person of character. I am responsible, dependable, reliable, honest, giving, loving, energetic and enthusiastic! All qualities I divinely inherited.

_____

_____

_____

_____

_____

_____

_____

_____

_____

_____

_____

_____

_____

_____

_____

_____

_____

_____

_____

_____

_____

_____

"All power is given unto me in heaven and earth."

—Matthew 28:18

What I think about I experience. I think good things.

_____

_____

_____

_____

_____

_____

_____

_____

_____

_____

_____

_____

_____

_____

_____

_____

_____

_____

_____

_____

_____

_____

_____

_____

_____

_____

"Now we have received, not the spirit of the world, but the spirit which is of God; that we might know the things that are freely given to us of God."

—1 Corinthians 2:12

I choose and attract friends of quality because I am a quality friend.

_____

_____

_____

_____

_____

_____

_____

_____

_____

_____

_____

_____

_____

_____

_____

_____

_____

_____

_____

_____

_____

_____

_____

_____

_____

_____

_____

"God…richly provides us with everything."

—1 Timothy 6:17

~ 14 ~

True power is not in controlling others or in having more than they have. It is in aligning myself with my inner Greatness and making a positive difference in the world around me.

_____

_____

_____

_____

_____

_____

_____

_____

_____

_____

_____

_____

_____

_____

_____

_____

_____

_____

_____

_____

_____

_____

_____

_____

_____

_____

_____

_____

"Christ the power of God, and the wisdom of God."
—1 Corinthians 1:24

When I do things the best way possible, I may not have to fix them later.

_____

_____

_____

_____

_____

_____

_____

_____

_____

_____

_____

_____

_____

_____

_____

_____

_____

_____

_____

_____

_____

_____

_____

_____

"Commit to the Lord whatever you do and your plans will succeed."
—Proverbs 16:3

I have the inner qualities of a winner. I am now the winner I was born to be.

"And you shall know the truth, and the truth shall make you free."
—John 8:32

I am not alone in my feelings. Many others feel or have felt exactly the same way. I express and release my feelings in a healthy and constructive way. Healing takes place where I need to heal.

"...the Lord my God will enlighten my darkness."

Anger is natural. There are lots of healthy ways to express it, such as exercising and talking out my feelings. I am always in control.

_____

_____

_____

_____

_____

_____

_____

_____

_____

_____

_____

_____

_____

_____

_____

_____

_____

_____

_____

_____

_____

_____

_____

_____

_____

_____

"A fool shows his annoyance at once, but a prudent person overlooks an insult."

—Proverbs 12:16

I am worth more than a coastline of diamonds and gold. My real worth is infinite. I am priceless. I treat myself that way.

_____
_____
_____
_____
_____
_____
_____
_____
_____
_____
_____
_____
_____
_____
_____
_____
_____
_____
_____
_____
_____
_____
_____
_____
_____
_____
_____

"For where your treasure is, there your heart will be also."
—Matthew 6:21

True givingness makes me rich in many ways.

_____
_____
_____
_____
_____
_____
_____
_____
_____
_____
_____
_____
_____
_____
_____
_____
_____
_____
_____
_____
_____
_____
_____
_____
_____

"Give, and it will be given to you."

—Luke 6:38

I believe.

_____

_____

_____

_____

_____

_____

_____

_____

_____

_____

_____

_____

_____

_____

_____

_____

_____

_____

_____

_____

_____

_____

_____

_____

_____

_____

_____

"All things can be done for the one who believes."

—*Mark 9:23*

If I can dream it, I can achieve it! I now have the patience and the perseverance to see my dream become a reality. I steadily work toward my goals. Action takes me there!

_____
_____
_____
_____
_____
_____
_____
_____
_____
_____
_____
_____
_____
_____
_____
_____
_____
_____
_____
_____
_____
_____
_____
_____
_____

"According to the grace of God given to me, like a skilled master builder I laid a foundation."

—1 Corinthians 3:10

I listen to the still God voice within, which tells me everything I need to know or where I can find the answers. I ask it questions, I get answers.

_____
_____
_____
_____
_____
_____
_____
_____
_____
_____
_____
_____
_____
_____
_____
_____
_____
_____
_____
_____
_____
_____
_____
_____
_____

"And all things, whatsoever you ask in prayer, believing, you shall receive."

—Matthew 21:22

I write the questions I need answers for here.

_____

_____

_____

_____

_____

_____

_____

_____

_____

_____

_____

_____

_____

_____

_____

_____

_____

_____

_____

_____

_____

_____

_____

_____

_____

_____

"My help comes from the Lord, who made heaven and earth."
—Psalm 121:2

I write the answers here (to my questions) as they come.

_____

_____

_____

_____

_____

_____

_____

_____

_____

_____

_____

_____

_____

_____

_____

_____

_____

_____

_____

_____

_____

_____

_____

_____

_____

"...the Father that dwelleth in me, he doeth the works.."

—John 14:10

I write more answers here (to my questions) as they come.

_____

_____

_____

_____

_____

_____

_____

_____

_____

_____

_____

_____

_____

_____

_____

_____

_____

_____

_____

_____

_____

_____

_____

_____

_____

_____

_____

"...the Father that dwelleth in me, he doeth the works.."

—John 14:10

When I am kind to others, I am kind to myself. My kindness has a ripple effect in the world.

"...where the Spirit of the Lord is, there is liberty."
—2 Corinthians 3:17

The commitment I make now to my faith is 100 percent. Anything less than that is not an option. My Oneness with God is rock solid.

_____

_____

_____

_____

_____

_____

_____

_____

_____

_____

_____

_____

_____

_____

_____

_____

_____

_____

_____

_____

_____

_____

_____

_____

"I will never leave you or forsake you."

—Hebrew 13:5

How attractive I am depends upon how I feel about myself inside. I say and think nice things about me.

_____

_____

_____

_____

_____

_____

_____

_____

_____

_____

_____

_____

_____

_____

_____

_____

_____

_____

_____

_____

_____

_____

_____

_____

_____

"A new heart will I give you, and a new spirit will I put within you..."

—Ezekiel 36:26

My parent(s) and I have a good relationship made of mutual respect and love. We listen to and understand each other.

_____

_____

_____

_____

_____

_____

_____

_____

_____

_____

_____

_____

_____

_____

_____

_____

_____

_____

_____

_____

_____

_____

_____

_____

_____

_____

"The meditation of my heart shall be understanding."

—*Psalm 49:3*

When I judge other people I am really judging myself. I accept others the way they are. The only one I need to change is me.

_____

_____

_____

_____

_____

_____

_____

_____

_____

_____

_____

_____

_____

_____

_____

_____

_____

_____

_____

_____

_____

_____

_____

"...be of good comfort, be of one mind, live in peace; and the God of love and peace shall be with you."

—2 Corinthians 13:11

I am made from the same Greatness which made the sun, the stars, the moon, the beaches and the forests. I Am.

_____

_____

_____

_____

_____

_____

_____

_____

_____

_____

_____

_____

_____

_____

_____

_____

_____

_____

_____

_____

_____

_____

_____

_____

"...the Kingdom of God does not come with observation; Neither shall they say, see here! or see there! For, behold the kingdom of God is within you."

—Luke 17:20-21

I am no less or no more than anyone else. I see God's Greatness in everyone I meet.

_____

_____

_____

_____

_____

_____

_____

_____

_____

_____

_____

_____

_____

_____

_____

_____

_____

_____

_____

_____

_____

_____

_____

_____

_____

_____

_____

"The Christ in me, meets the Christ in you."

—A favorite quote

I have the freedom to choose. I make excellent choices. I learn from all the choices I make. Every choice contributes to my wholeness.

"Show me your ways, O Lord; teach me your paths."

—Psalm 25:4

I have the strength to say yes.

_____
_____
_____
_____
_____
_____
_____
_____
_____
_____
_____
_____
_____
_____
_____
_____
_____
_____
_____
_____
_____
_____
_____

"Let your yes be yes..."

—*James 5:12*

I have the strength to say no.

"...and let your no be no."

—James 5:12

I can be cool without doing things for the sake of being accepted. I choose to do what's safe and healthy for me. God always accepts me.

_____

_____

_____

_____

_____

_____

_____

_____

_____

_____

_____

_____

_____

_____

_____

_____

_____

_____

_____

_____

_____

_____

_____

_____

_____

"God is love; and he who abides in love abides in God, and God in him."

—1 John 4:16

I have the strength to be my own person. God strengthens me now.

"But the Lord made the heavens. Honor and majesty are before him; strength and joy are in his place."

—*1 Chronicles 16:26-27*

There isn't a substance in the world that can give me a better high than giving, caring and loving can. These gifts provide me with a natural high for living.

_____
_____
_____
_____
_____
_____
_____
_____
_____
_____
_____
_____
_____
_____
_____
_____
_____
_____
_____
_____
_____
_____
_____
_____
_____
_____

"Or do you not know that your body is the temple of the Holy Spirit who is in you? ...therefore Glorify God in your body."
—*1 Corinthians 6:19,20*

If conflict arises, rather than resisting the person or situation, I encircle them and myself with light and love. Love is powerful. It heals and resolves.

_____

_____

_____

_____

_____

_____

_____

_____

_____

_____

_____

_____

_____

_____

_____

_____

_____

_____

_____

_____

_____

_____

_____

"A soft answer turneth away wrath; but grievous words stir up anger."

—Proverbs 15:1

I set realistic goals for the day, week, month and year. These goals lead me to my Ultimate or Bigger goals.

_____

_____

_____

_____

_____

_____

_____

_____

_____

_____

_____

_____

_____

_____

_____

_____

_____

_____

_____

_____

_____

_____

_____

"He who looks into the perfect law of liberty and continues in it, and is not a forgetful hearer but a doer of the work, this one will be blessed in what he does."

—James 1:25

If I believe I can, I'm right. If I believe I can't, I'm also right. Which do I believe?

_____

_____

_____

_____

_____

_____

_____

_____

_____

_____

_____

_____

_____

_____

_____

_____

_____

_____

_____

_____

_____

_____

_____

_____

_____

_____

_____

_____

_____

"Pray in the Spirit at all times in every prayer and supplication. To that end keep alert and always persevere."

—Ephesians 6:18

Everyone loves a giver. I choose to be one. I am balanced in my giving and taking.

_____
_____
_____
_____
_____
_____
_____
_____
_____
_____
_____
_____
_____
_____
_____
_____
_____
_____
_____
_____
_____
_____
_____
_____
_____

"For with you is the fountain of life."

—Psalm 36:9

I worked hard to plant the seeds, now I joyfully reap the harvest. God, the Greatness within me, perseveres!

_____

_____

_____

_____

_____

_____

_____

_____

_____

_____

_____

_____

_____

_____

_____

_____

_____

_____

_____

_____

_____

_____

_____

"The farmer waits for the precious crop from the earth, being patient with it until it receives the early and late rains. You must also be patient."

—*James 5:7-8*

**Pessimism stunts my growth while optimism fuels it.
Anything is possible with my "can do" attitude!**

_____

_____

_____

_____

_____

_____

_____

_____

_____

_____

_____

_____

_____

_____

_____

_____

_____

_____

_____

_____

_____

_____

_____

_____

"Nothing shall be impossible unto you."

—Matthew 17:20

In the silence within, God whispers through my feelings what needs to be done and exactly how to do it.

_____

_____

_____

_____

_____

_____

_____

_____

_____

_____

_____

_____

_____

_____

_____

_____

_____

_____

_____

_____

_____

_____

_____

_____

_____

_____

"When you pray, go into your room, and when you have shut your door, pray to your Father who is in the secret place; and your Father who sees in secret will reward you openly."

—Matthew 6:6

I love my life. It is a precious gift.

_____

_____

_____

_____

_____

_____

_____

_____

_____

_____

_____

_____

_____

_____

_____

_____

_____

_____

_____

_____

_____

_____

_____

_____

_____

"Thanks be to God for His indescribable gift!"

—2 Corinthians 9:15

I do the best I can. God's Greatness within me does the rest.

_____

_____

_____

_____

_____

_____

_____

_____

_____

_____

_____

_____

_____

_____

_____

_____

_____

_____

_____

_____

_____

_____

_____

_____

_____

"Commit the way unto the Lord; trust also in Him: and He shall bring it to pass."

—Psalm 37:5

I can choose not to follow everyone else. I am secure enough in myself to know what is best for me. I am the leader of my life.

_____

_____

_____

_____

_____

_____

_____

_____

_____

_____

_____

_____

_____

_____

_____

_____

_____

_____

_____

_____

_____

_____

_____

"Be strong and of good courage; do not be afraid, nor dismayed, for the Lord your God is with you wherever you go."

—Joshua 1:9

I accept and expect the very best for me, which is unfolding and happening right now.

_____
_____
_____
_____
_____
_____
_____
_____
_____
_____
_____
_____
_____
_____
_____
_____
_____
_____
_____
_____
_____
_____
_____
_____
_____
_____
_____
_____
_____
_____

"Have faith in God."

—Mark 11:22

Daily I am guided to my Greatest Good.

_____

_____

_____

_____

_____

_____

_____

_____

_____

_____

_____

_____

_____

_____

_____

_____

_____

_____

_____

_____

_____

_____

_____

"And the Lord shall guide thee continually..."

—Isaiah 58:11

When I work or study first, I create free time that I can enjoy later. Taking action gives me freedom.

_____

_____

_____

_____

_____

_____

_____

_____

_____

_____

_____

_____

_____

_____

_____

_____

_____

_____

_____

_____

_____

_____

_____

_____

_____

_____

"The desire accomplished is sweet to the soul..."

—*Proverbs 13:19*

Action comes before motivation, not the other way around. With love and passion I take action on what I need or want to do.

_____

_____

_____

_____

_____

_____

_____

_____

_____

_____

_____

_____

_____

_____

_____

_____

_____

_____

_____

_____

_____

_____

_____

_____

_____

_____

_____

_____

"Let all things be done decently and in order."

—*1 Corinthians 14:40*

I have infinite potential because I am infinite potential.

_____

_____

_____

_____

_____

_____

_____

_____

_____

_____

_____

_____

_____

_____

_____

_____

_____

_____

_____

_____

_____

_____

_____

_____

_____

_____

*"Great is our Lord, and of great power; His understanding is
infinite."*

—Psalm 147:5

What can I do that will serve God, give others joy and give me happiness?

_____

_____

_____

_____

_____

_____

_____

_____

_____

_____

_____

_____

_____

_____

_____

_____

_____

_____

_____

_____

_____

_____

"In God I trust; I am not afraid."

—Psalm 56:4

God's Greatness within me is the source for all my Good.

_____

_____

_____

_____

_____

_____

_____

_____

_____

_____

_____

_____

_____

_____

_____

_____

_____

_____

_____

_____

_____

_____

_____

_____

_____

_____

"Behold, the Kingdom of God is within you."

—Luke 17:21

By giving thanks, I make room for more in my life. I give thanks to God for everything. I am truly blessed.

_____

_____

_____

_____

_____

_____

_____

_____

_____

_____

_____

_____

_____

_____

_____

_____

_____

_____

_____

_____

_____

_____

_____

_____

_____

"Every day I will bless thee..."

—*Psalm 145:2*

I have the strength to go the extra mile and accomplish what I've set out to do. I see amazing results because of this.

_____

_____

_____

_____

_____

_____

_____

_____

_____

_____

_____

_____

_____

_____

_____

_____

_____

_____

_____

_____

_____

_____

_____

_____

_____

_____

"For your steadfast love is before my eyes, and I walk in faithfulness to you."

—Psalm 26:3

What would I do if I were guaranteed success?

_____

_____

_____

_____

_____

_____

_____

_____

_____

_____

_____

_____

_____

_____

_____

_____

_____

_____

_____

_____

_____

_____

_____

_____

_____

"Remember that it is not you that supports the root, but the root that supports you."

—*Romans 11:18*

I do what I love. I strive for excellence in all that I do.

"Strive for the greater gifts. And I will show you a still more excellent way."

—1 Corinthians 12:31

I do what is necessary to heal any past hurts: talk, forgive, listen, read, write, play. Nothing stands between me and becoming more.

_____

_____

_____

_____

_____

_____

_____

_____

_____

_____

_____

_____

_____

_____

_____

_____

_____

_____

_____

_____

_____

_____

_____

_____

"Be renewed in the spirit of your minds."

—Ephesians 4:23

I have my perfect place on the team. I excel as an individual because I do what is best for my team. I'm a team player; my inner Greatness shines!

_____

_____

_____

_____

_____

_____

_____

_____

_____

_____

_____

_____

_____

_____

_____

_____

_____

_____

_____

_____

_____

_____

_____

_____

_____

"The disciples were filled with joy and with the Holy Spirit."
—Acts 13:52

**Younger and older people can be a wealth of knowledge.
I listen and learn from everyone.**

_____

_____

_____

_____

_____

_____

_____

_____

_____

_____

_____

_____

_____

_____

_____

_____

_____

_____

_____

_____

_____

"Love never ends."

—1 Corinthians 13:8

If at times my feelings and emotions feel like they are upside down, I recognize this period of time is essential for my growth. I am kind to me. God is right where I am.

_____

_____

_____

_____

_____

_____

_____

_____

_____

_____

_____

_____

_____

_____

_____

_____

_____

_____

_____

_____

_____

_____

_____

_____

"Then your light shall break forth like the morning and your healing shall spring forth speedily."

—Isaiah 58:8

I organize and motivate a group to clean a beach or a park.
We also plant trees and flowers. I love and respect the earth.

_____

_____

_____

_____

_____

_____

_____

_____

_____

_____

_____

_____

_____

_____

_____

_____

_____

_____

_____

_____

_____

_____

"Choose this day whom you will serve."
—Joshua 24:15

I do everything in moderation, I am a well-balanced person.

_____

_____

_____

_____

_____

_____

_____

_____

_____

_____

_____

_____

_____

_____

_____

_____

_____

_____

_____

_____

_____

_____

_____

_____

"You show me the path of life."

—Psalm 16:11

~ 67 ~

I relax and let go as my inner Greatness guides me into perfect accomplishment in all that I do.

_____

_____

_____

_____

_____

_____

_____

_____

_____

_____

_____

_____

_____

_____

_____

_____

_____

_____

_____

_____

_____

"I will strengthen you, I will help you."
—Isaiah 41:10

I am a peaceful person, inwardly and outwardly.

"Be still and know that I am God..."

—Psalm 46:10

My faith in myself and the Greatness within me grows stronger with each passing day.

_____

_____

_____

_____

_____

_____

_____

_____

_____

_____

_____

_____

_____

_____

_____

_____

_____

_____

_____

_____

_____

_____

_____

_____

_____

"...According to your faith be it unto you."
                    —Matthew 9:29

When I look in the mirror I recognize God's Greatness within me. I accept and love all of who I am.

"...in quietness and confidence shall be your strength."
—Isaiah 30:15

I am a positive example for someone who is younger than I.

_____
_____
_____
_____
_____
_____
_____
_____
_____
_____
_____
_____
_____
_____
_____
_____
_____
_____
_____
_____
_____
_____

"A cheerful heart has a continual feast."

—Proverbs 15:15

If I think of something negative which I don't like, I quickly affirm the positive in its place. If it bothers me too much I write it down and write the positive next to it. I see the truth in this and in all matters.

_____
_____
_____
_____
_____
_____
_____
_____
_____
_____
_____
_____
_____
_____
_____
_____
_____
_____
_____
_____
_____
_____
_____
_____

"...Behold, I make all things new."

—*Revelation 21:5*

If I am increasingly uncomfortable in a relationship I'm in, I give myself permission to move on. I bless and release the person with love to his or her Highest Good.

_____

_____

_____

_____

_____

_____

_____

_____

_____

_____

_____

_____

_____

_____

_____

_____

_____

_____

_____

_____

_____

_____

"And uphold me by your generous Spirit."
—Psalm 51:12

The past is gone. It has no power over me. I accept this new day and the wonderful things it brings.

_____

_____

_____

_____

_____

_____

_____

_____

_____

_____

_____

_____

_____

_____

_____

_____

_____

_____

_____

_____

_____

_____

_____

_____

_____

_____

_____

_____

"Create in me a clean heart, O God; and renew a right spirit within me."

—Psalm 51:10

When I greet people I look them in the eyes and speak with confidence. God's inner Greatness shines. I have every reason to be confident.

_____

_____

_____

_____

_____

_____

_____

_____

_____

_____

_____

_____

_____

_____

_____

_____

_____

_____

_____

_____

_____

_____

_____

_____

"You are the light of the world."

—*Matthew 5:14*

I have many talents and continue to develop many more.

_____

_____

_____

_____

_____

_____

_____

_____

_____

_____

_____

_____

_____

_____

_____

_____

_____

_____

_____

_____

_____

_____

_____

_____

_____

_____

"...Christ in you, the hope of glory..."
—*Colossians 1:27*

There is a power for Good in the world. I effectively use it in my life.

_____

_____

_____

_____

_____

_____

_____

_____

_____

_____

_____

_____

_____

_____

_____

_____

_____

_____

_____

_____

_____

_____

_____

_____

_____

_____

"God saw everything that He had made, and indeed, it was very good."

—Genesis 1:31

Whatever my ethnicity, my religion, my country, my language or how much I have, I am proud to be me.

_____

_____

_____

_____

_____

_____

_____

_____

_____

_____

_____

_____

_____

_____

_____

_____

_____

_____

_____

_____

_____

_____

_____

_____

_____

"The light is with you."

—John 12:35

There is a Divine Plan for my life. I was made in God's image and likeness. I have all the tools I need to live successfully.

_____

_____

_____

_____

_____

_____

_____

_____

_____

_____

_____

_____

_____

_____

_____

_____

_____

_____

_____

_____

_____

_____

_____

"God is my strength and power: and he maketh my way perfect."
                                                    —2 Samuel 22:33

Success is not just fame or fortune. Those things are fine. Real success is in doing Good. Making a positive difference...that's success!

_____

_____

_____

_____

_____

_____

_____

_____

_____

_____

_____

_____

_____

_____

_____

_____

_____

_____

_____

_____

_____

_____

_____

_____

_____

"Like good stewards of the manifold grace of God, serve one another with whatever gift each of you has received."

—*1 Peter 4:10*

I hear and understand what you are saying. I listen with my mind and my heart.

_____

_____

_____

_____

_____

_____

_____

_____

_____

_____

_____

_____

_____

_____

_____

_____

_____

_____

_____

_____

_____

_____

"Wisdom rests quietly in the heart of him who has understanding."
—Proverbs 14:33

What I say to someone can directly affect their day.
I say kind and positive things in a sincere way.

_____
_____
_____
_____
_____
_____
_____
_____
_____
_____
_____
_____
_____
_____
_____
_____
_____
_____
_____
_____
_____
_____
_____
_____

"In the beginning was the Word...and the word was made flesh..."
—John 1:1, 14

I picture in my mind exactly who I want to be. I feel what it's like to be the true me. God guides me in becoming who I am.

_____

_____

_____

_____

_____

_____

_____

_____

_____

_____

_____

_____

_____

_____

_____

_____

_____

_____

_____

_____

_____

_____

_____

_____

_____

"Call to Me, and I will answer you, and show you great and mighty things, which you do not know."

—Jeremiah 33:3

If I feel tired or feel as though I don't have the strength to do what I need to do, I relax and allow God to work through me. I can do it!

_____

_____

_____

_____

_____

_____

_____

_____

_____

_____

_____

_____

_____

_____

_____

_____

_____

_____

_____

_____

_____

_____

_____

_____

_____

_____

"...they that wait upon the Lord shall renew their strength...."
—Isaiah 40:31

The food I eat is blessed and converted into energy. Every fiber of my being is healthy, strong, and filled with love.

_____

_____

_____

_____

_____

_____

_____

_____

_____

_____

_____

_____

_____

_____

_____

_____

_____

_____

_____

_____

_____

_____

"By this we know that we abide in Him, and He in us, because He has given us of His Spirit."

—1 John 4:13

I am kind and loving. My relationships are in perfect harmony. God, through me, blesses everyone I meet. I am fun and pleasant to be around.

_____
_____
_____
_____
_____
_____
_____
_____
_____
_____
_____
_____
_____
_____
_____
_____
_____
_____
_____
_____
_____
_____
_____
_____
_____

"...every one that loveth is born of God, and knoweth God."
—1 John 4:7

I release feeling rushed. Where am I rushing to anyway? I do more by being poised and relaxed. I do only what's realistic for the present moment. All things get done. I look at how much I've done at the end of each day!

_____
_____
_____
_____
_____
_____
_____
_____
_____
_____
_____
_____
_____
_____
_____
_____
_____
_____
_____
_____
_____
_____

"This I know, that God is for me.... In God I trust."

—Psalm 56:9, 11

I treat my things with care. I find they last much longer that way.

_____

_____

_____

_____

_____

_____

_____

_____

_____

_____

_____

_____

_____

_____

_____

_____

_____

_____

_____

_____

_____

_____

_____

_____

"And walk in love..."

—*Ephesians 5:2*

~ 89 ~

My inner beauty sparkles like a sunlit waterfall.

_____

_____

_____

_____

_____

_____

_____

_____

_____

_____

_____

_____

_____

_____

_____

_____

_____

_____

_____

_____

_____

_____

_____

_____

"Surely God is in thee..."

—Isaiah 45:14

I am the rich loving child of the Greatness within, around and through me, the Creator of all life.

"...and he which soweth bountifully shall reap also bountifully."
—2 Corinthians 9:6

What are my fears?

_____

_____

_____

_____

_____

_____

_____

_____

_____

_____

_____

_____

_____

_____

_____

_____

_____

_____

_____

_____

_____

_____

_____

"For God hath not given us the spirit of fear; but of power, and of love, and of a sound mind."

—2 Timothy 7:7

When I give, I give from the heart. I don't expect anything in return. God is the only Source for all of my needs.

_____

_____

_____

_____

_____

_____

_____

_____

_____

_____

_____

_____

_____

_____

_____

_____

_____

_____

_____

_____

_____

_____

_____

"The Lord is my shepherd; I shall not want."
                                        —Psalm 23:1

I am aware of time. My intuition guides me to use it effectively.

"To set the mind on the Spirit is life and peace."
—Romans 8:6

I love without worrying about being loved. Love works in my life much more easily this way.

"...let us not love in word, neither in tongue; but in deed and in truth."

—1 John 3:18

I am the captain of my own life-ship. I steer it anywhere I want to go by my thoughts, words and actions. The sea of God's Greatness flows divinely through me, carrying me to my destiny. I do my part, God does the rest.

_____

_____

_____

_____

_____

_____

_____

_____

_____

_____

_____

_____

_____

_____

_____

_____

_____

_____

_____

_____

_____

_____

_____

_____

_____

"For all the promises of God in Him are Yes; to the glory of God through us."

—2 Corinthians 1:20

I am divinely guided to the perfect school or work. God knows exactly where I belong and prepares the way. I find it's perfect for me, better than I could have imagined!

"He has filled the hungry with good things."
—_Luke 1:53_

I have the ability to make good decisions and choices.
I am decisive. The Greatness within me knows exactly what
to do at all times.

_____

_____

_____

_____

_____

_____

_____

_____

_____

_____

_____

_____

_____

_____

_____

_____

_____

_____

_____

_____

_____

_____

"You hold my right hand. You guide me with your counsel."
—*Psalm 73:23-24*

I am the Olympian of my own life. The gold is within my reach. I simply claim it and accept it. It belongs to me!

"...if therefore thine eye be single, thy whole body shall be full of light."

—*Matthew 6:22*

I learn about things that interest me. I excel in those things that excite me!

_____
_____
_____
_____
_____
_____
_____
_____
_____
_____
_____
_____
_____
_____
_____
_____
_____
_____
_____
_____
_____
_____
_____
_____

"Serve the Lord with gladness: come before his presence with singing."

—Psalm 100:2

**When I take tests or exams, I prepare for them wisely.
I envision myself knowing and writing the answers.
I expect and receive the highest marks.**

_____

_____

_____

_____

_____

_____

_____

_____

_____

_____

_____

_____

_____

_____

_____

_____

_____

_____

_____

_____

_____

_____

_____

*"The Lord helps them and delivers them...because they take refuge
in Him."*

—Psalm 37:40

The Greatness within me guides me to excellent grades. My positive and loving attitude shines through to my teachers. It's cool to do well. I accept this for me.

_____

_____

_____

_____

_____

_____

_____

_____

_____

_____

_____

_____

_____

_____

_____

_____

_____

_____

_____

_____

_____

_____

_____

_____

_____

"That all the peoples of the earth may know that the Lord is God; there is no other."

—*1 Kings 8:60*

**If I sense others are envious of my good and success,
I silently bless them and know it is okay for me to succeed.**

"...the Lord is the strength of my life; of whom shall I be afraid?"
—Psalm 27:1

I am whole and complete right at this very moment.

"...be of good comfort; thy faith hath made thee whole."
—Matthew 9:22

**Patience is a quality of my inner Greatness. My patience
and perseverance pays off...big time.**

_____

_____

_____

_____

_____

_____

_____

_____

_____

_____

_____

_____

_____

_____

_____

_____

_____

_____

_____

_____

_____

_____

_____

_____

_____

_____

*"Wait on the Lord; be of good courage, and He shall strengthen your
heart."*

—Psalm 27:14

The world is my oyster. I am the pearl.

_____

_____

_____

_____

_____

_____

_____

_____

_____

_____

_____

_____

_____

_____

_____

_____

_____

_____

_____

_____

_____

_____

_____

"You are precious in my sight..."

—Isaiah 43:4

Creativity bubbles up from the wellsprings of my being in an endless flow of Good, constantly supplying me with brilliant ideas.

"It is God who giveth us richly all things to enjoy."

I give in all areas of my life, especially to my spiritual sources. This activity brings a constant flow of Good to my life. It also gives me health and peace of mind.

_____

_____

_____

_____

_____

_____

_____

_____

_____

_____

_____

_____

_____

_____

_____

_____

_____

_____

_____

_____

_____

_____

_____

_____

_____

_____

_____

"The tithe of all things brought they in abundantly...and laid them by heaps at the alter."

—*2 Chronicles 31:5, 6*

I can still say what I need to say to someone I love who has passed on. This person lives forever in my heart and memory.

_____

_____

_____

_____

_____

_____

_____

_____

_____

_____

_____

_____

_____

_____

_____

_____

_____

_____

_____

_____

_____

_____

_____

_____

"I thank God upon every rememberance of you..."
—Philippians 1:3

I always remember who I am, where I am from and where I am going.

_____

_____

_____

_____

_____

_____

_____

_____

_____

_____

_____

_____

_____

_____

_____

_____

_____

_____

_____

_____

_____

_____

_____

"A good name is more desirable than great riches..."

—Proverbs 22:1

There are millions of loving, kind, giving, caring people who believe in the possibility of a better world. I join them in making it a reality.

_____

_____

_____

_____

_____

_____

_____

_____

_____

_____

_____

_____

_____

_____

_____

_____

_____

_____

_____

_____

_____

"...the earth is full of the goodness of the Lord."

—*Psalm 33:5*

~ 111 ~

The burning fire (of energy) in my desires and dreams turns into a blazing fire of success. I am passionate!

"Awake, my soul! Awake!"

—Psalm 57:8

I accept my Divine inheritance. I am thankful!

"...I have come that they might have life, and that they might have it more abundantly."

—_John 10:10_

I live my life in beautiful living color. My personality is vibrant and very attractive!

_____
_____
_____
_____
_____
_____
_____
_____
_____
_____
_____
_____
_____
_____
_____
_____
_____
_____
_____
_____
_____
_____
_____
_____
_____
_____

"Ye shall know them by their fruits."

—Matthew 7:16

With kind words and actions, I help those who are hurting. The Greatness in me brings out the Greatness in them. Healing takes place.

_____

_____

_____

_____

_____

_____

_____

_____

_____

_____

_____

_____

_____

_____

_____

_____

_____

_____

_____

_____

_____

_____

_____

"Our God and Father of all, who is above all, through all, and in you all."

—Ephesians 4:6

I think and dwell on the solution, not the problem. Life works wonders this way. What is the solution to the thing that has been on my mind lately?

_____

_____

_____

_____

_____

_____

_____

_____

_____

_____

_____

_____

_____

_____

_____

_____

_____

_____

_____

_____

_____

_____

_____

"I will lift up my eyes unto the hills, from whence comes my help."
—Psalm 121:1

I Am.

_____

_____

_____

_____

_____

_____

_____

_____

_____

_____

_____

_____

_____

_____

_____

_____

_____

_____

_____

_____

_____

_____

_____

_____

_____

"God said to Moses, I Am who I Am."

—Exodus 3:14

I am safe wherever I go. I allow God's Holy Spirit to protect me. I am attuned to Divine Guidance.

_____

_____

_____

_____

_____

_____

_____

_____

_____

_____

_____

_____

_____

_____

_____

_____

_____

_____

_____

_____

_____

_____

"You will be protected and take your rest in safety."

—Job 11:18

Love is the ultimate healing power. I love my enemies as well as my friends. I see powerful transformations in my relationships and they are Good.

_____

_____

_____

_____

_____

_____

_____

_____

_____

_____

_____

_____

_____

_____

_____

_____

_____

_____

_____

_____

_____

_____

_____

_____

"Beloved, let us love one another."

—1 John 4:7

I refuse to buy into false images I see on television, in magazines, and in movies. I am perfectly confident, comfortable and happy being me.

_____

_____

_____

_____

_____

_____

_____

_____

_____

_____

_____

_____

_____

_____

_____

_____

_____

_____

_____

_____

_____

_____

"In the world you shall have tribulation; but be of good cheer, I have overcome the world."

—*John 16:33*

Happiness is within me. It is a frame of mind—an attitude, one I adopt and keep.

_____

_____

_____

_____

_____

_____

_____

_____

_____

_____

_____

_____

_____

_____

_____

_____

_____

_____

_____

_____

_____

_____

_____

_____

_____

_____

"Clap your hands, all you peoples; shout to God with loud songs of joy."

—Psalm 47:1

Grudges, pain and resentment block me from my Good. They have no place in my heart. I lovingly release and dissolve them into the nothingness from where they came.

_____

_____

_____

_____

_____

_____

_____

_____

_____

_____

_____

_____

_____

_____

_____

_____

_____

_____

_____

_____

_____

_____

"And be ye kind to one another, tender hearted, forgiving one another, even as God...hath forgiven you."

—Ephesians 4:32

There is nothing within me that can keep me from my Greatest Good. No one else's negative words have any power over me. I am free to think positively for myself. I am free and unlimited right now.

_____

_____

_____

_____

_____

_____

_____

_____

_____

_____

_____

_____

_____

_____

_____

_____

_____

_____

_____

_____

_____

_____

_____

_____

_____

"You did not choose Me, but I chose you and appointed you that you should go and bear fruit."

—John 15:16

I focus on the thing I am doing. If other thoughts come, I can write them down and act on them later. There is power in commitment. There is power in accomplishment.

_____

_____

_____

_____

_____

_____

_____

_____

_____

_____

_____

_____

_____

_____

_____

_____

_____

_____

_____

_____

_____

_____

_____

_____

_____

"Jesus said, 'For mortals it is impossible, but for God all things are possible.'"

—*Matthew 19:26*

Life is learning. It would be very boring if we knew everything. What challenge would *that* be?

_____

_____

_____

_____

_____

_____

_____

_____

_____

_____

_____

_____

_____

_____

_____

_____

_____

_____

_____

_____

_____

_____

_____

_____

_____

"Lead me in your truth, and teach me, for you are the God of my salvation."

—*Psalm 25:5*

God's Greatness tree for me is already planted. All I need to do is care for it, water it, love it, and nurture it. God does the rest.

_____

_____

_____

_____

_____

_____

_____

_____

_____

_____

_____

_____

_____

_____

_____

_____

_____

_____

_____

_____

_____

_____

"They are like trees planted by streams of water, which yield their fruit in its season, and their leaves do not wither."

—Psalm 1:3

I no longer fear rejection. I am not rejectable. I am a loving child of God.

_____

_____

_____

_____

_____

_____

_____

_____

_____

_____

_____

_____

_____

_____

_____

_____

_____

_____

_____

_____

_____

_____

_____

"The light shines in the darkness, and the darkness has not overcome it."

—*John 1:5*

When it seems like I can't go on and I have to give up, that is
the hour of greatest promise, to prove my faith in God and in
myself.

_____

_____

_____

_____

_____

_____

_____

_____

_____

_____

_____

_____

_____

_____

_____

_____

_____

_____

_____

_____

_____

_____

"Nothing shall be impossible unto you."
—Matthew 17:20

I am thankful everyday for everything in my life, big or small, that God has provided.

_____

_____

_____

_____

_____

_____

_____

_____

_____

_____

_____

_____

_____

_____

_____

_____

_____

_____

_____

_____

_____

_____

_____

_____

"Let us come into His presence with thanksgiving: let us make a joyful noise to Him with songs of praise!"

—Psalm 95:2

How do I feel about love?

_____

_____

_____

_____

_____

_____

_____

_____

_____

_____

_____

_____

_____

_____

_____

_____

_____

_____

_____

_____

_____

_____

_____

"See what love the Father has given us, that we should be called children of God; and that is what we are."

—1 John 3:1

How do I feel about my parents?

_____
_____
_____
_____
_____
_____
_____
_____
_____
_____
_____
_____
_____
_____
_____
_____
_____
_____
_____
_____
_____
_____
_____
_____

"I am praying for them...for they are thine."

—John 17:9

How do I feel about my family?

_____

_____

_____

_____

_____

_____

_____

_____

_____

_____

_____

_____

_____

_____

_____

_____

_____

_____

_____

_____

_____

_____

_____

_____

"Let us work for the good of all, and especially for those of the family of faith."

—Galatians 6:10

How do I feel about my teachers?

_____

_____

_____

_____

_____

_____

_____

_____

_____

_____

_____

_____

_____

_____

_____

_____

_____

_____

_____

_____

_____

_____

"As He was setting out on a journey, a man ran up and knelt before Him, and asked Him, 'Good Teacher, what must I do to inherit eternal life?'"

—*Mark 10:17*

How do I feel about my relationships?

_____

_____

_____

_____

_____

_____

_____

_____

_____

_____

_____

_____

_____

_____

_____

_____

_____

_____

_____

_____

_____

_____

_____

_____

_____

_____

"...whatsoever things are true...honest...just...pure...lovely...think on these things."

—Philippians 4:8

~ 134 ~

How do I feel about my past, present and future?

_____

_____

_____

_____

_____

_____

_____

_____

_____

_____

_____

_____

_____

_____

_____

_____

_____

_____

_____

_____

_____

_____

_____

"If I take the wings of the morning, and dwell in the uttermost parts of the sea; Even there shall thy hand lead me, and thy right hand shall hold me..."

—Psalm 139:9, 10

How can I turn a burden into a blessing?

_____

_____

_____

_____

_____

_____

_____

_____

_____

_____

_____

_____

_____

_____

_____

_____

_____

_____

_____

_____

_____

_____

"The tongue of the wise brings healing."
—*Proverbs 12:18*

What can I do that will make a difference?

_____

_____

_____

_____

_____

_____

_____

_____

_____

_____

_____

_____

_____

_____

_____

_____

_____

_____

_____

_____

_____

_____

_____

_____

_____

*"And after the earthquake a fire; but the Lord was not in the fire:
and after the fire a still small voice."*

—1 Kings 19:12

What can I do today that will affect my life for the better tomorrow?

_____

_____

_____

_____

_____

_____

_____

_____

_____

_____

_____

_____

_____

_____

_____

_____

_____

_____

_____

_____

_____

_____

_____

_____

_____

"I will counsel you with my eye upon you."
—*Psalm 32:8*

What are the things that really connect me to me? Which places in nature do I feel most connected?

_____

_____

_____

_____

_____

_____

_____

_____

_____

_____

_____

_____

_____

_____

_____

_____

_____

_____

_____

_____

_____

_____

_____

"Come away to a deserted place all by yourselves and rest a while."
—*Mark 6:31*

Thank you pages (on these pages I write everything I am thankful for.)

_____

_____

_____

_____

_____

_____

_____

_____

_____

_____

_____

_____

_____

_____

_____

_____

_____

_____

_____

_____

_____

_____

_____

_____

_____

"Enter His gates with thanksgiving."

—Psalm 100:4

Another thank you page...

_____

_____

_____

_____

_____

_____

_____

_____

_____

_____

_____

_____

_____

_____

_____

_____

_____

_____

_____

_____

_____

_____

_____

_____

_____

"Do not worry about anything, but in everything by prayer and supplication with thanksgiving let your request be made known to God."

—Philippians 4:6

To order

God's Greatness Is Within Me!

Please call 1-800-684-1313

or

Mail $9.95 plus $3.00 s+h

(+ 5% Massachusetts Sales Tax if applicable)

to: Lighthouse Publications

27 S. Monroe Terrace, Suite #4000

Boston, Massachusetts 02122

allow 5-15 days for delivery

QUANTITY DISCOUNTS AVAILABLE

Churches, Groups & Organizations
can purchase these journals in quantity.

Please call 1-800-684-1313
for more information.

Thank You!